Science Fair Success Using the Internet, Revised and Updated

Marc Alan Rosner

Enslow Publishers, Inc.

40 Industrial Road	PO Box 38
Box 398	Aldershot
Berkeley Heights, NJ 07922	Hants GU12 6BP
USA	UK

http://www.enslow.com

Dedication

I dedicate this book to my daughters and nephews,
for whom every day is a science project.

Library of Congress Cataloging-in-Publication Data

Rosner, Marc Alan.
    Science fair success using the Internet / Marc Alan Rosner.— 2nd ed., rev. and updated.
      p. cm. — (Science fair success)
    Includes bibliographical references and index.
    ISBN 0-7660-2425-3 (hardcover)
    1. Science projects—Data processing—Juvenile literature. 2. Internet—Juvenile
literature. I. Title. II. Series.
    Q182.3.R68   2005
    507.8—dc22
                               2005006749

Printed in the United States of America

10 9 8 7 6 5 4 3 2 1

To Our Readers: We have done our best to make sure all Internet Addresses in this book were active and appropriate when we went to press. However, the author and the publisher have no control over and assume no liability for the material available on those Internet sites or on other Web sites they may link to. Any comments or suggestions can be sent by e-mail to comments@enslow.com or to the address on the back cover.

Illustration Credits: © 1997–2005 Annenberg/CPB, p. 106; © 2001 Miami Museum of Science, p. 92; © 2005 CDLI, p. 15; © 2005 Google, pp. 20, 30; Copyright © 1994–2005 by William A. Arnett, p. 77; Copyright © 1995, 1995, 1997, 1998, 1999, 2000 The Center for Astrophysical Research in Antarctica., p.72; Copyright © 1996–2005 Yinon Bentor, p. 97; Copyright © 1998–1999; All Rights Reserved, Anthony Capri, p. 43; Copyright © 2002–2004 David M. Harrison, p. 105; Copyright © 2004 University of North Dakota, p. 65; Copyright © 2005 Yahoo! Inc, pp. 13, 17; Hazelwood School District (Florissant, MO), p. 99.

Cover Photo: © IT Stock

Revised edition of *Science Fair Success Using the Internet*, Copyright © 1999.

Contents

Introduction

Computers are useful tools if you have a science project to complete. In fact, scientists invented computers and the Internet to solve problems. This book is about using the Internet to create an interesting, interactive science project. Of course you can use your computer as a word processor or to download pictures. But you can also use the most modern and interesting Web sites for learning. You can communicate directly with scientists on the cutting edge of research.

Modern personal computers are many times more powerful than their ancestors. Computers arrived in homes and classrooms relatively recently. In the late 1970s, you could place your telephone handset on a simple modem, and your computer would find a link to the outside world. Today, you can use a home computer with a modem to surf the World Wide Web. You can read text, view pictures, hear sounds, and watch video. You can interact with the many millions of other people connected to the Internet—all in a much faster and more sophisticated way than before.

The opening chapters of this book get you online with valuable research tips and strategies. Each of the following chapters covers a different area of science. The chapters start with an example of a science project that uses the Internet in some way. Then it lists the best Web sites pertaining to the chapter's topic.

In this book you will learn how to use the Internet to help you choose your science project and how to make it unique and personal. As you do your research, you will learn to be creative and make decisions. Internet-based research can make your project more in-depth and up-to-date. Your finished project will reveal important things about science and you.

Are you willing to spend time online? Do you want to build your technical skills? Are you committed to a serious work schedule over several weeks? If so, then read on. If you follow the steps in this book, you will be able to build a project that will make you, your teacher, and your family proud.

A Note on Web Sites

Web sites are nothing more than files that you access on someone else's computer. When you type a Web address (URL) in your Web browser, you are directing your computer to connect to a specific place on the Internet. Web sites frequently move as people change the way they store and provide information. If you find that any of the Web addresses in this book are no longer accurate, try searching for the title of the Web site in Google or another search engine; very often this will lead you to the new site.

Chapter 1

Using the Internet for Science Projects and Research

What exactly is the Internet? The Internet is many computers linked together electronically. When you visit a Web site, send an e-mail, or download a file, you are exchanging information between one computer and another. Government and university scientists developed the Internet in the late 1960s so that they could share research findings. In 1990, a group of Swiss researchers developed the World Wide Web, a method for viewing the information on one computer from another using text and graphics. This change helped bring today's explosion in computer use. Internet usage more than doubled between the years 2000 and 2004, and it continues to grow rapidly.

Families and schools have found a much faster connection to the Internet through broadband devices such as cable modems and fiber optic data lines. Think of information flowing to and from your computer on a wide highway rather than on a country road.

How Can I Use the Internet for My Project?

You can use the Internet to support your research. Instead of using the World Wide Web *as* your project, use it to *enhance* your project.

Examples of good Internet use include:

- Gathering and analyzing data from a weather site over two weeks.
- Learning about animal species in a far-off rain forest so that you can design a food web.

Examples of poor Internet use include:

- Printing many pages from a Web site and mounting them on poster board.
- Linking quotes from different sources with no explanation and no references.

Project Preparation

How do you complete a science project? How do you even start one? Intricate, thought-provoking assignments scare some people. Science projects are big jobs that have to be done over a period of weeks or months. The trick is to break your project down into little pieces. In choosing your project, start with what interests you.

Let's examine how Kimberly, an imaginary student, chooses and develops her project. Kimberly is an eighth-grade physical science student at Sherman Middle School. She has been assigned a two-month project. It must relate to physics, chemistry, or earth science. She must follow a scientific method and make a project proposal. When it is approved, she must show her data and write a rough draft of her science project report. Then she must make a clear, final draft and enter it in her school's science fair in a presentable manner. She has these deadlines:

February 15: Project proposal due.
March 1: Show initial data.
March 15: Rough draft of report due.
April 1: Final draft of report due.
April 7: Enter project in science fair for judging.

Kimberly is not worried about this schedule. She will break her project into parts and meet each deadline. In choosing a project, she thinks about her interests. She has always been fascinated by weather. When she was little, she was in a hurricane with her family in Florida. Ever since then, she has followed news reports about storms and unusual weather events. She likes to watch the weather change. She asks her parents many questions about the atmosphere and ocean. When they cannot give answers, she asks her teacher. She knows she wants to research this topic. She knows she can take measurements of temperature and humidity. She might even be able to predict the weather.

Kimberly has a computer she wants to use to support her research. Her first step will be to narrow down her topic and make a proposal.

Before Kimberly begins her research, she will establish some safety rules that all students should follow. There are two sets of guidelines, one for Internet use and the other for the project itself.

Safe Computing

The Internet can put you in touch with strangers. Kimberly knows she must use good judgment. She will follow these rules:

- Do not give personal information such as your last name, address, or telephone number to anyone.

- Do not name your school or friends without permission from your teacher and parents.

- If anyone you contact acts in an inappropriate way, tell a parent or teacher immediately. The adult can report the occurrence to your online service and other authorities.

- Read and follow the rules of your online service.

- Never give your password to anyone.

- Never give out other private information such as your credit card number or social security number. Your online service already has this information.

- Download and print files only when necessary.

- Use antivirus software to protect your computer.

Safe Experimenting

There is a chance Kimberly will handle equipment, chemicals, or glassware during her project. She wants to be safe, so she will wear protective clothing and work in a proper laboratory when necessary. Her teacher will advise her on safety issues. And Kimberly will follow these rules:

- Follow the instructions for conducting this project. Plan your work with a teacher, including safety procedures.

- Obey the rules of the classroom and laboratory.

- Wear safety goggles with side protection when handling chemicals, glass, or fast-moving objects.

- Handle chemicals in proper containers.

- Mix chemicals following proper instruction; never change quantities or substitute other chemicals.

- Use a fume hood and a well-ventilated laboratory when necessary.

- Be careful with electricity, especially when near water, and experiment with electricity only under the supervision of a knowledgeable adult.

- Do not eat or drink while experimenting.

- Review the operation of laboratory safety equipment such as eye wash and fire extinguishers.

- Report any laboratory accidents, spills, or injuries to a teacher.

- Take note when an experiment calls for adult supervision.

Logging On to the Information Highway

This book will not teach you how to access the Internet. If you do not yet know how to browse the World Wide Web, you can get a book on that topic. When you are comfortable "surfing the Net," you will be prepared to continue.

Kimberly has a personal computer at home she will use for Internet access. Her school science lab and library also have computers with World Wide Web access. Her home computer has 256 megabytes of RAM, a 2.4-gigahertz processor, a 40-gigabyte hard drive, and a cable modem. (Lower numbers than these would make her work slower, but still possible.) She subscribes to an online service that provides e-mail and a Web browser. A *Web browser* is a program that allows you to view graphics on the Internet.

Here are a few recommendations for using Internet Explorer and other browsers:

1. Use the most modern browser your computer can support. The newer the version, the better it will support useful features such as Java, Quicktime, Windows Media Player, and Shockwave, which are called *plug-ins.* Many sites use these features, and more and more require them for the best performance.

2. Bookmark useful sites (add them to your Favorites) so that you can visit them again without searching.

3. Highlight selected text in a browser window, then copy and paste it into a word processing program such as Microsoft Word or ClarisWorks. Be sure to highlight, copy, and paste into your document the Web address where you found the text.

4. Try to work early in the morning, when computer use is low. The Internet will be fast and you won't be competing with family members to use the computer.

5. Learn advanced features of your computer and software. Examples of this include:

   • Adjusting the "preferences" in your software programs.

   • Learning to save information from one program into the format of another.

   • Scanning an image to include it in a slide show.

Choosing a Project

Kimberly is prepared to take the first step in her project: choosing a topic. She decides that the World Wide Web might

A Web browser allows you to see graphics on the Internet. Yahoo! is one of many Web search engines that contain graphics.

13

be a useful place to start, so she visits some sites related to science projects to get ideas. The first one she goes to is:

Science Fairs Home Page
http://www.cdli.ca/sciencefairs/

This home page has listings of science project ideas at all levels and in all science areas.

Kimberly clicks on "Intermediate Projects" and finds project ideas for her grade level. She scrolls down the page and finds fifteen different project ideas under "meteorology," including:

1. Snow—What happens when it melts; what it contains; structure of snowflakes; life in a snowbank.

2. Sky Color—Account for differences in color at different times.

3. Wind and Clouds—What are the common wind patterns in your area and why.

At this point Kimberly thinks it might be interesting if she recorded weather-related measurements at her home and tried to make predictions.

Many individuals and schools have made their project ideas available on the Web. Here are some other science project sites where you can find and share ideas:

Cyber-Fair: Steps to Prepare a Science Fair Project
http://www.isd77.k12.mn.us/resources/cf/steps.html

Discoveryschool.com: Science Fair Central
http://school.discovery.com/sciencefaircentral/

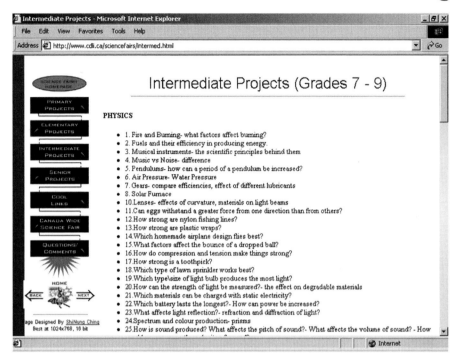

To see a list of project ideas, go to the "Science Fairs Homepage" site. You may get an idea to start your own original project.

Internet Public Library: Science Fair Project Resource Guide

http://www.ipl.org/div/kidspace/projectguide/

Science Buddies

http://www.sciencebuddies.org/

The Science Club

http://scienceclub.org/

Science Hobbyist

http://www.eskimo.com/~billb/

The WWW Virtual Library: Science Fairs

http://physics.usc.edu/~gould/ScienceFairs/

Some sites, such as the following one, charge a membership fee for full access.

Science Project

http://www.scienceproject.com/

Although it is not necessary to join a fee-based site, you can browse it for ideas. Your school library may have access to some online research services; ask your school librarian to point you in the right direction.

Here are some general Web sites for science education:

Cornell University, Cornell Theory Center: Math and Science Gateway

http://www.tc.cornell.edu/CTC-Main/Services/Education/
Gateways/Math_and_Science/

Exploratorium: The Museum of Science, Art and Human Perception

http://www.exploratorium.edu/

Frank Potter's Science Gems

http://www.sciencegems.com/

The Lab-ABC's Gateway to Online Science

http://www.abc.net.au/science/default.htm

SciEd: Science and Mathematics Education Resources

http://newton.physics.wwu.edu:8082/jstewart/scied/science.
html

Scientific American
http://www.sciam.com/
> *Each of these sites leads to resources in the different branches of science.*

Searching for Useful Web Sites
Once Kimberly chooses her general topic, she is ready to do a search for useful Web sites. She starts by going to this search service:

Yahooligans! The Web Guide for Kids
http://www.yahooligans.com/

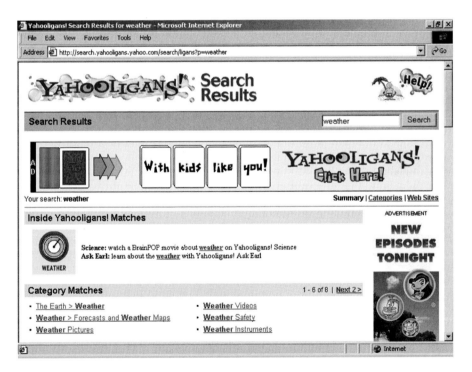

By entering the word *weather* into the Yahooligans! search engine, Kimberly found many sites that had relevant information she might be able to use for her science fair project.

She enters the word "weather" and clicks the Search button. The computer provides her with eight categories and 149 sites. She can visit those weather-related resources by clicking on anything that is *hot text*, that is, colored and underlined. The *categories* are groups of Web sites in the Yahoo! search service. The *sites* are direct links to Web resources on weather.

Kimberly uses the mouse to click on the suggestions from Yahooligans! She finds a wide range of weather sites. Some have weather forecasts, while others are about storms and natural disasters. Many suggest science experiments for students. A few are useful, but most are not. Kimberly understands that people create Web sites for all sorts of reasons. Some sites are designed to share information, and others to sell products. Some are meant to express opinions. It is her job to decide which are reliable and relevant to her project. Her parents and teacher help her do this.

Kimberly notes which sites are useful. She bookmarks the good ones in the menu of her Web browser (she adds them to her Favorites) so that she can easily return to them later. She also makes a few notes with pen and paper so that she will remember what her favorite sites contain. This is a very important stage of research: sifting through all the information to get at what is useful.

It is important to understand that Yahooligans! is a search engine. *Search engines* are Web sites that list other sites. They allow you to enter a keyword to research a specific topic. The search engine does not contain the information you need, it merely points you in the right direction. Search engines are to the Internet what card catalogs are to libraries. Using both the

Internet and the library will make your project stronger. Other search services you might visit are these:

Education World
http://www.education-world.com/

Google Kids & Teens
http://directory.google.com/Top/Kids_and_Teens/

KidsClick
http://www.kidsclick.org/

To find other search engines appropriate for students, go to the following:

Kid's Search Engines
http://searchenginewatch.com/links/article.php/2156191

These are more advanced search engines :

Altavista
http://www.altavista.com

Google
http://www.google.com

Yahoo!
http://www.yahoo.com/

Meta-search engines compile results from several search engines at once. They also have advanced search features. Examples include:

Ask Jeeves for Kids
http://www.ajkids.com/

Dogpile
http://www.dogpile.com

Metacrawler
http://www.metacrawler.com

Searching Tips

Here are some important tips for using search engines:

1. Read the instructions for each search engine.

2. Do not be afraid to surf around, checking out many sites before deciding which ones are useful. Make sure to visit several of the sites that come up.

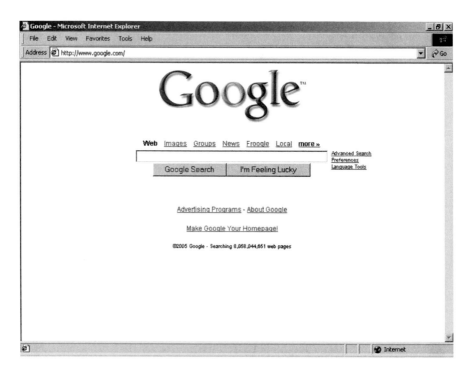

Google is a search engine you can use to find Web sites that will help you research your science topic.

3. Internet sites are not all the same quality. You can trust an Internet site hosted by the American Museum of Natural History (http://www.amnh.org) more than one created by an America Online user with a personal account. In general, U.S. university (ending in ".edu") and government (ending in ".gov") Web sites are reliable.

4. If you find a useful site, bookmark it with your Favorites in your browser so that you do not lose it; it can be hard to find later if you forget how you got there. There are tens of millions of Web sites now!

5. If you do not find a useful site on your first attempt, or if you find too many sites, modify your query using different word combinations. Kimberly's first search in Yahooligans! for "weather" produced eight categories and 149 sites. When she searched for "weather events," she got no categories and five sites.

6. Try different search engines to see which work best for you. They work differently. Some search engines list their sites because of human recommendations. Some search engines prowl the Web and find sites that match the words you are searching for.

7. Learn the rules for each search engine. A search for *weather measurements* in Google gave over a million pages. A search for "weather measurements" in quotes gave under five thousand. The difference? The first search gave all the Web sites it knew with the word *weather* or *measurements*. The second gave only those sites with that exact sequence of words.

Conducting an Experiment:
The Scientific Method

Kimberly wants to design and carry out a good experiment. To do this, she uses the scientific method. First she poses a problem or question. Then she decides what kinds of experiments will help her find the answer. Using the results of her experiments, she will be able to draw a conclusion for her question.

Problem or question. What do you want to show? What questions do you want your project to answer? Kimberly decides on this question: "What factors determine the weather?" Often, the researcher follows the question with a hypothesis. A hypothesis is an explanation or a best guess at answering the question at hand. Then the experiment is conducted to try to prove the hypothesis.

Experiment design. What equipment and materials will you use to collect data, and how will you do it? Kimberly intends to take measurements the way a meteorologist would. She finds three sites that give information on how to take measurements from weather maps and with other equipment:

Athena Curriculum: Weather
http://vathena.arc.nasa.gov/curric/weather/hsweathr/

Franklin Institute: Make Your Own Weather Station
http://www.fi.edu/weather/todo/todo.html

USA Today Weather Measurements
http://www.usatoday.com/weather/resources/basics/measurements.htm

Kimberly decides to record temperature, air pressure, and dew point every day outside her home for four weeks. She will take her measurements in the same way at the same time each day.

Soon after starting her work, Kimberly arrives at this hypothesis: "A drop in air pressure leads to stormy weather." She forms this hypothesis from both her own data and from her Internet research.

Results. The results include your data, with relevant tables, graphs, and calculations. Since Kimberly has a Macintosh computer, she decides to make her tables, graphs, and report using AppleWorks. (A classmate of hers does the same thing with a Windows-based Dell computer using Microsoft Office.) Kimberly is able to cut and paste her tables and graphs into her report. She also uses her school's computer lab to print them out large and in color. She mounts the most important graphs on poster board for presentation in the science fair.

Conclusion. What does your research show? What would you do to continue your research if you had more time? Kimberly finds that when the air pressure drops significantly over a twenty-four-hour period, the weather usually turns stormy. Sudden drops in air pressure come with wind and rain. This agrees with the information and theories she finds at general weather sites such as these:

Intellicast
http://www.intellicast.com/

UM Weather
http://cirrus.sprl.umich.edu/wxnet/

USA Today Weather
http://www.usatoday.com/weather/wfront.htm

The Weather Channel
http://www.weather.com/

Kimberly follows the steps of the scientific method. She meets with her teacher a few times to show her the data she is collecting and to make sure she is on track. She spends time preparing her science fair entry. She uses large poster board to present her findings.

Of course, if your teacher provides a format for the scientific method that is somewhat different from this one, you should follow your teacher's format closely. Some projects, such as those that involve interviews or computer programming, might have a different set of steps. The following sites will help with the scientific method. They offer tips on creating science projects, including the various stages (making observations, gathering information, and coming up with a title and hypothesis, etc.); sample projects; and presentation tips.

Experimental Science Projects: An Introductory-Level Guide
http://www.isd77.k12.mn.us/resources/cf/SciProjIntro.html

Science Fair Project on the Web
http://sciencefairproject.virtualave.net/

Other weather sites are listed on pages 64–66.

Chapter 2

Communicating Using the Internet

The Internet is useful not only for the information it contains but also for the people with whom you may want to communicate. This chapter explores various ways to contact people online and gives you guidelines for online communication.

Message Boards

Message boards are areas within online services where people post electronic messages about specific topics. There are message boards on gardening, collecting coins, and investment; and there are message boards on science education and science projects. At home, Kimberly subscribed to America Online (AOL), so she logged on to AOL and entered Keyword [command-k] "message boards." This brought her to Message Board Central on the service. She clicked on Search Boards and entered "weather projects." She entered "weather science projects," and eighty-four messages came up in her search.

Some of the messages were not useful to her. For instance, several messages were from people who were traveling and wanted to know about the weather in other places. Several messages, however, caught her eye; they were from other students researching their own projects. Most of these were on the "Ask-A-Teacher Homework Help" board in the middle school science fair area.

Message Boards ⇒
Ask-A-Teacher Homework Help ⇒
Middle School ⇒
Sciences 6–8 ⇒
Science Fair

Here she was able to read the messages of students and the answers given by teachers. Remember, the Internet is a vast collection of information. Much of what you find will not be useful. Some of it will. You have the job of deciding what information you can trust and how to use it. Kimberly decided it would be a good idea to post a message herself. First she read the Message Board FAQs. *FAQ* stands for "Frequently Asked Questions." On the Message Board FAQs, she found instructions on how to use electronic forums.

Before she posted her question, she spent some time reading the many messages already in the folder. To her surprise, some of her questions had already been asked and answered! After spending time browsing this area, she composed a question of her own and posted it:

Subj: Weather Forecast Help
Date: 2/20/05 7:02:23 PM
From: KimberlyT85
Hi,
    I'm doing a project for school on weather. I want to take measurements near my home and forecast the weather. I'm looking for suggestions about what measurements to take and how to analyze them. I know I want to measure temperature and rainfall, but what else? What patterns should I look for? I already bought a thermometer and rain gauge, and I'm studying weather on the World Wide Web. My project rough draft is due in about a month.
Thank you.

Notice the strong points of Kimberly's request. She did not demand help, she asked politely. She was very specific in her request. She showed that she already started her research and is trying on her own. Imagine if she posted it this way:

Subj: Help me PLEEZ!
Date: 2/20/05 7:02:23 PM
From: KimberlyT85
    Hey! I know lots of teachers and sceintists are out there. Can anyone tell me how to do my weather project? Its twenty-five percent of my grade this term!

If you were a busy professional, which message would you answer?

Newsgroups

Newsgroups, also known as forums, bulletin boards, and roundtables, bring together people who share the same interest. Newsgroup messages remain on the Web for all to see, even nonmembers. They are basically the largest electronic bulletin boards in the world. They are an effective research tool because you can see the record of electronic conversations that have taken place over time between interested participants. Check the Frequently Asked Questions (FAQ) file for your newsgroup. You may find that someone has already answered some of your questions. As with all your sources, cite newsgroups if you get information from them for your project.

You can find a directory of newsgroups through your online service or Web browser or on the World Wide Web at such sites as this one:

Google Groups
http://groups-beta.google.com/

The groups with the prefix "sci." are dedicated to science. There are many specific subgroups dedicated to the different disciplines in science. Here are some examples:

NEWSGROUP	TOPIC OF DISCUSSION
sci.bio.botany	botany
sci.chem.electrochem.battery	batteries
sci.optics.fiber	fiber optics
sci.energy.hydrogen	hydrogen as a fuel source
sci.geo.meteorology	weather
sci.bio.ecology	ecological environments (e.g., coral reefs)

Kimberly was having difficulty figuring out how to measure humidity. She knew it was important to her project, so she went to the Google group for weather and did a keyword search for "humidity."

Many messages came up. One in particular caught her eye. It was titled "Humidity: Part 1 of 4" and seemed to be related to her question. The following posting came up when she clicked on the title:

> Relative humidity (RH) is the ratio of the density of the water vapor in the air at any temperature to the density that would exist if the air were saturated with water vapor at that temperature.

This was a good start, but she did not understand how one would measure humidity, so she refined her search to "how do I measure humidity." Then she saw an answer to someone else who had asked the same question:

> Subject: Re: how to measure humidity
> What would be a reasonably inexpensive way to measure humidity? Well, they have these neat little gizmos called hygrometers now. They are like a thermometer, only they measure humidity. Can get them at pretty much any DIY [Do-It-Yourself] type store in various formats and qualities.

With further research she found the following:

> On measuring humidity—Woodcraft (www.woodcraft.com) sells a hygrometer (about 2.5" diameter) for under eight dollars. . . . The woodcraft hygrometer is good-looking and accurate, and just the right size (inexpensive too!). Note: The www.woodcraft.com site has a catalog online. There are other sources for inexpensive accurate hygrometers—you do not have to pay fifteen or twenty dollars for one.

Kimberly used this information to shop for a humidity meter.

E-Mail

E-mail stands for "electronic mail." It is a way of sending a written message to someone by computer. To do this you need an e-mail account, which you can get through your online service, school, or certain free Web sites such as Yahoo! mail (http://mail.yahoo.com). E-mail is a good way to communicate in modern times. It is fast. It saves paper. You can store your messages and replies easily.

Sometimes people send e-mail without checking for proper grammar or spelling. Sometimes they are impolite. Do not make these mistakes. Do not send any message that you would be uncomfortable sending by regular mail or reading aloud in person. And always show your best side when sending mail to

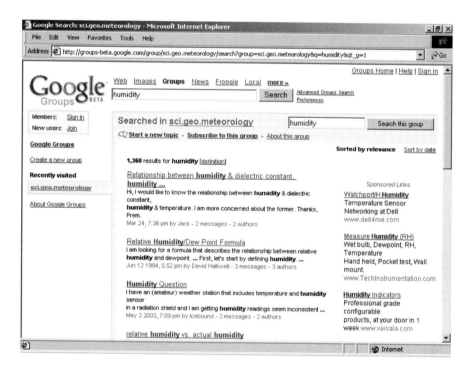

Kimberly did a keyword search in a Google group to help her find messages relating to measuring humidity.

a respected professional or someone you do not know. If you act serious, you will be taken seriously.

Online services provide their own instructions for using e-mail. Here are some ideas on how you can use this powerful and modern method of communication to reach scientists who might help you with a project.

Contacting Scientists Online

One of the ways you can use the Internet in a science project is to reach scientists. Although scientists are very busy people who often work long hours and receive dozens of messages a day, they enjoy sharing their knowledge with interested students. It is important that you contact them only after you have worked on your project for a while. You want to get their attention and let them know that you have made an effort to learn on your own and that you have a genuine interest in their research. When should you ask a scientist a question? Ask yourself these questions first:

1. Was I unable to answer the question on my own, even after trying?

2. Is this person an expert who could provide specific information in this area?

If you answer yes to both questions, it might be worthwhile for you to contact this scientist.

Before you ask the scientist a question, carefully read the instructions at the site. You may find that someone has already asked your question and the answer is posted online. If you still feel it would be worthwhile to ask your question, then go ahead—just be sure to compose it carefully.

Kimberly posed a question to a meteorologist she found on the Web:

Date: February 20, 2005 11:19:58 A.M.
Subj: Request for Science Project Assistance
To: PFeingold@weather.feinlab.com

Dear Dr. Feingold,
I found your name in the Scientists-Helping-Students Web site. I hope you can take the time to answer a question I have. I'm trying to forecast my local weather. So far I have started measuring air temperature, pressure, and humidity every day. I know that a drop in air pressure can indicate bad weather. But how far does it have to drop, and how fast, for a storm to form? I could not find this information in my school library or on the Web. Since you are a meteorologist and do research, you might have more experience in this area. If I hear from you within two weeks, I can use your answer to support my project. Thank you for your time. I hope to find out more about what you do.

Sincerely,
Kimberly
E-Mail: KimberlyT85@aol.com

To summarize, your message should be very specific and should contain the following important features:

- *Who* you are (but do not give your last name).

- *What* you want to know, and what you have already learned on your own.

- *Why* you are asking this person for help.

- *When* you need the information.
- A polite and professional tone.

It does *not* contain:

- A vague question.
- A demand for assistance.
- Errors in spelling or grammar.
- Insufficient time for the scientist to respond.
- Your telephone number, home address, or other personal information.

Here is another tip: People generally enjoy talking about their work. Ask them about their research, and they will usually tell you all about it. This will help with your research. And when you do get a reply, the following are essential:

1. Thank them immediately and let them know they have helped you.

2. Cite them in your research as a source (see pages 37–39).

Here are some of the many Web sites on which you may pose questions to scientists:

Ask a Biologist
http://askabiologist.asu.edu/

Ask a Geologist
http://walrus.wr.usgs.gov/ask-a-geologist/

Ask a High Energy Scientist
http://imagine.gsfc.nasa.gov/docs/ask_astro/
ask_an_astronomer.html

Ask a Mad Scientist
http://www.madsci.org/submit.html

Ask Dr. Science
http://www.drscience.com/

CIESE General Ask-An-Expert Web Sites
http://www.k12science.org/askanexpert.html

Howard Hughes Medical Institute (Biology)
http://www.hhmi.org/askascientist/

How Things Work
http://howthingswork.virginia.edu/home.html

OMSI Science Whatzit!
http://www.omsi.edu/explore/whatzit/

SchoolWide Zoo Experts
http://www.schoolworld.asn.au/species/expert.html

Scientific American Ask the Experts
http://www.sciam.com/askexpert_directory.cfm

USA Today Weather Questions Answered
http://www.usatoday.com/weather/resources/askjack/wjack3.
htm

You are not limited to these sites. Many scientists have their own Web sites or work for laboratories or research institutions that have Web sites. You can find them by searching online or by contacting universities or government institutions. These Web sites almost always have an e-mail link. Click the link to send a message to one of the scientists or to the site administrator.

Mailing Lists

People join mailing lists with others who share an interest. This kind of list is called a *listserv*. When a member sends a message to the listserv, the message automatically goes out to all the members. There are mailing lists for all types of interests, including specific scientific fields of study. Every listserv has a list of FAQs that you should consult when you join. Think carefully before you send out messages to listservs. Some have thousands of members. An adult should approve any message you send. It is an excellent idea to monitor the listserv for a week or so before you send any messages, to learn the culture of the group.

Using listservs is an advanced Internet skill and should be done with help from an adult. Most listservs are targeted for graduate students and adults.

Kimberly used Google (www.google.com) to search for "weather listserv." The first item that came up was:

WEATHER@LISTSERV.CMICH.EDU
http://www.lsoft.com/scripts/wl.exe?SL1=WEATHER&H=LISTSERV.CMICH.EDU

This is the Central Michigan University listserv on weather. It has instructions on how to join the listserv and how to contact the person who runs it.

E-Zines and Magazines

E-zines are electronic magazines. New e-zines are launched each month, and many are free. Sometimes newsstand magazines have Web sites that offer some of their content for free. These sites are worth exploring for their articles, images, and forums:

Discover Magazine
http://www.discover.com/

Nature
http://www.nature.com/

Science Daily
http://www.sciencedaily.com/

Science Magazine
http://www.sciencemag.org/

Science News
http://www.sciencenews.org/

Scientific American
http://www.sciam.com

Yahoo's directory of science magazines is organized by popularity; its categories are listed alphabetically:

Yahoo Directory of Science Magazines
http://dir.yahoo.com/Science/News_and_Media/Magazines/

Cite Your References

As with any essay or term paper, it is essential for you to cite your research sources, whether you quote someone directly or rephrase their words or ideas. You probably already know that you must cite references to books and magazines using footnotes and a bibliography—by presenting title, author, and publication information. But how do you cite Internet sources?

Kimberly found a good quote on barometric pressure and hurricanes she wanted to use. Notice how she presented her information:

> "In North America, barometric measurements at sea level seldom go below 29 inches of mercury (982 millibars), and in the tropics it is generally close to 30 inches (1,016 millibars) under normal conditions. Hurricanes drop the bottom out of those normal categories. The Labor Day hurricane that struck the Florida Keys in 1935 had a central pressure of only 26.35 inches (892 millibars). And the change is swift: Pressure may drop an inch (34 millibars) per mile."
> [Leon County Division of Emergency Management (LCDEM), (1997). "Hurricane Survival Guide," Available Online: http://www.co.leon.fl.us/lcem/ anatom.htm (2005, March 2)].

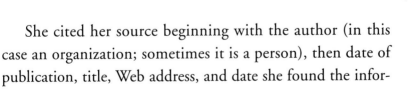

She cited her source beginning with the author (in this case an organization; sometimes it is a person), then date of publication, title, Web address, and date she found the information.

To cite newsgroup and e-mail sources, give the author of the message, date it was posted, subject of message, name of discussion list, and date you found it. For instance, look at how Kimberly presented her reply from Dr. Feingold:

"Dear Kimberly,
In my experience, a drop of over 10 millibars per hour for more than three hours indicates a bad storm is on the way. Of course this depends on the time of year and the geographic location. Hurricanes are more likely to form in certain regions where they can be warmed by ocean water, such as coastal Florida. You may use actual data from our research station in your report. You will find it at <http://www.weather.feinlab.com/data/hurrcane.html> [Dr. Terry Feingold, "Request for Science Project Assistance," e-mail dated February 25, 2005.]

If you want to learn more about how to cite software and Web sites, check these addresses:

APA Electronic References
http://www.apastyle.org/elecgeneral.html

Columbia Guide to Online Style
http://www.columbia.edu/cu/cup/cgos/idx_basic.html

Online! Citation Styles
http://www.bedfordstmartins.com/online/citex.html

The most important thing is that when you use someone else's work for your research, you give them credit. Give enough information for your reader to find your original source. Your teacher may give you a format to follow. Do not be afraid to ask for help. In general, your research will yield more reliable results when you use several Web sites, comparing and contrasting your findings, rather than simply taking quotes and images from one place.

Producing a Web Site of Your Own

At the completion of your project, you may want to create a Web site of your own to share with the world. Most online services have instructions on how to create Web pages. This can be part of your project.

More and more schools are getting modems and computer networks. You might be able to bring in your files on a floppy, CD, or Zip disk. Or you might bring a laptop computer to school, with a security cable to keep it in place.

Your teacher may be able to help you publish your work on the school's Web site. Make sure when you use the computers at your school that you observe your school's Acceptable Use Policy (AUP).

Chapter 3

Biology Projects Using the Internet

Kevin was assigned a seventh-grade life sciences project. He chose to do a project on cells, the building blocks of tissue in plants and animals. Because cells are so small, scientists view them with microscopes. Optical microscopes use lenses. Other microscopes, such as electron microscopes, give different (and sometimes clearer) images of cells and cell parts. Viewing cells under a microscope in biology class, Kevin found their appearance very interesting.

The main question Kevin sought to answer was: How does the type of light source affect plant cell development? Kevin hypothesized that the plants would grow best under a light source like sunlight, which is a mixture of different wavelengths of radiation. He planned on growing cells under five different lighting conditions:

- fluorescent light

- incandescent light

- grow light

- sunlight

- darkness

Kevin bought the lightbulbs he needed from a lighting store. He grew two types of plants—peas and tomato plants—under each type of light. (His teacher helped him decide which cells to use and how to prepare them.) He collected tissue samples from different stages of development, mounted them, stained them, and created labeled sketches of the cells and their parts. Through this method he showed that the plants with the healthiest and most developed cells had grown under the light sources most similar to sunlight. The plants grown in darkness and under incandescent light had cells that were smaller and irregular in formation.

Kevin wanted his project to show the structure and function of cell organelles, or cell parts. *Structure* refers to the composition, shape, and position of the organelle—what it *is*. *Function* is what the organelle *does*, how it keeps the cell alive and makes it work. Structure and function are very important to biologists, especially those who study cells, anatomy, and evolution. To make his project interesting and informative, Kevin used different materials in his presentation:

- A working microscope with some cell samples.

- Sketches of cells and labeled diagrams, made by hand.

- Photographs of cells, taken with a camera that adapted to the microscope in his science class.

- Models of a plant cell made from common household materials such as cardboard, foam, and dried pasta.

- Images of cells from the World Wide Web.

Kevin did not use the Web for all his cell images, only for those images that he had trouble producing on his own. For instance, his microscope was not powerful enough to show ribosomes, which are very small. He had to present them in a different way.

Kevin did some Web searches for cells and cell-related terms. He used terms such as "cell," "ribosomes," "virtual cell," "organelles," and "nucleus," entering these keywords in the search engines. He found this site early in his search:

Cells

http://www.visionlearning.com/library/module_viewer. php?c3=&mid=64&l=

The opening page of this site provided an overview of the cell and an explanation of its parts. After reading the information and looking at some cell images, he scrolled down. He saw a section called "Resources" and clicked on "Animal Cell." This displayed an easy-to-read diagram of a cell with its different organelles labeled. After studying the cells parts, he printed the color diagram for his report. Then he checked out the links to other cell websites.

Kevin found useful images of individual cell parts on this site:

Cells Alive!

http://www.cellsalive.com/

The opening page of this site provided a directory of the site contents. He clicked on "Plant Cell." This brought him

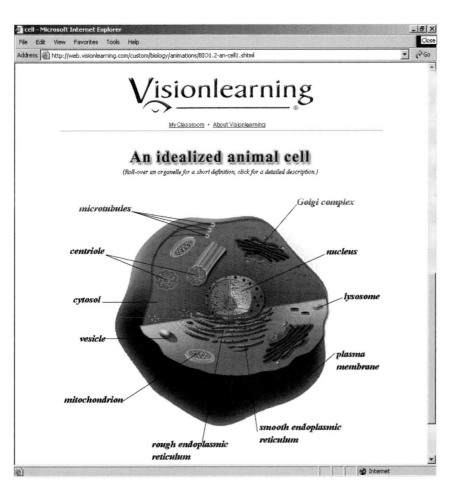

An idealized animal cell
(Roll-over an organelle for a short definition, click for a detailed description.)

microtubules

Golgi complex

centriole

nucleus

cytosol

lysosome

vesicle

plasma membrane

mitochondrion

smooth endoplasmic reticulum

rough endoplasmic reticulum

Images of cells and their parts can be found on the Internet to enhance a cell biology project.

to a picture of plant cells with the different organelles labeled. When he clicked on a particular organelle, it brought him to a detailed description of that cell part. He was able to wander through this site as if he were walking through the rooms of a house. He printed the color images he needed to fill out his report.

Kevin's project was successful. He showed the relationship between variable light and the development of plant cells. He identified some differences between animal and plant cells. For instance, plant cells have chlorophyll and animal cells do not. Plant cells also have more rigid cell walls. Kevin used a few images from the Internet. Most of what he displayed, however, was of his own creation. He included his own sketches, photographs, and models.

Other Sites to Help You in Your Biology Research

Animal Anatomy

Cats

http://www.nationalgeographic.com/features/97/cats/

At this National Geographic site, you can learn about the anatomy of cats. You can study their muscular and skeletal structures, examine the way they sense things, and learn how they behave individually and in groups.

ChickScope

http://chickscope.beckman.uiuc.edu/

ChickScope has great images of chicken embryology. It contains over 2,000 MRI images and explanations of how MRIs work and how you can use the images to learn.

The Exploratorium's Cow's Eye Dissection

http://www.exploratorium.edu/learning_studio/cow_eye/index.html

At this site you can follow a virtual cow eye dissection on the Web.

NetFrog Digital Dissection

http://curry.edschool.Virginia.EDU/go/frog

The Virtual Frog Dissection Kit Version 2.2

http://froggy.lbl.gov/virtual/

These two sites allow you to "dissect" a virtual frog. You can learn about anatomy without actually harming a frog. You can slice open your digital frog and examine the tissues and organs of these amphibians.

Whole Frog Project

http://froggy.lbl.gov/

This is the main Web site for the Whole Frog Project, where you can examine images and movies of frogs and frog parts in virtual reality.

Animal Studies

Conchologist's Information Network

http://www.conchologistsofamerica.org/home/

If you collect shells, you will enjoy this site. You can identify different types of marine creatures here. There is a detailed reference list for gastropod information.

The Gator Hole
http://home.cfl.rr.com/gatorhole/
Alligators are feared and often misunderstood by humans. At the Gator Hole, you can set the record straight by separating the myths from the facts. Learn about alligator biology: its anatomy, feeding habits, and reproductive methods.

Exploring Hide & Seek
http://www.units.muohio.edu/dragonfly/hide/index.htmlx
Camouflage is an important wild animal survival strategy. These activities deal with camouflage.

How Wolves Communicate
http://www.units.muohio.edu/dragonfly/com/
This site analyzes how wolves communicate in a pack. It describes their strategies for establishing roles and marking territory. Then it leads to a way to analyze your own pets' behavior.

Iowa State University Entomology Image Gallery
http://www.ent.iastate.edu/imagegallery/
This site has many images from a large collection of insects. If you are interested in the world's smaller creatures, learn about beetles, lice, butterflies, moths, cicadas, leafhoppers, and other insects here. You can collect insects from your home area, preserve them in clear containers of rubbing

alcohol, and use printouts from the image gallery to enhance your study. Science stores sell insect containers or kits with built-in magnifying lenses.

Monarch Watch

http://www.monarchwatch.org/

This award-winning Web site teaches about the world of monarch butterflies. You can do a study of their ecological niche and migration patterns. There is also information on milkweed plants; use the site's handy photo guide to identify milkweed in your area, or find out how to grow your own plants.

National Zoological Park Home Page

http://nationalzoo.si.edu/

You can use this site to support animal study. It can help you create a profile of the animal: What does it eat? Where does it sleep? What predators should it avoid? What strategies does it use to protect itself? Is it endangered? How has it adapted to the presence of humans?

The Nutty Birdwatcher

http://www.birdnature.com/

This site is all about birds and birdwatching. You can learn about the different species of birds, find instructions for building a nest box, learn how to feed and identify birds in your own yard, and learn about their survival needs.

USGS Biological Resources

http://biology.usgs.gov/

This is another site for animal enthusiasts. It will direct you to relevant libraries, organizations, projects and programs, fact sheets, current research, photos, stories, and educational areas.

USGS Patuxent Wildlife Research Center

http://www.pwrc.usgs.gov/

The Patuxent Wildlife Research Center was founded in 1936 as America's first wildlife experiment station and research refuge. You can get involved in the specific monitoring of amphibians, birds, butterflies, and other species at this site.

WhaleNet at Wheelock College, Boston

http://whale.wheelock.edu/Welcome.html

Whale Songs

http://www.whalesongs.org/

These two whale sites have sections designed for students.

Wonders of the Seas

http://www.oceanicresearch.org/lesson.html

This is a growing collection of lessons on sponges, mollusks, and many other creatures of the sea. It contains facts and diagrams describing the anatomy of these organisms, where they live, how they feed, and what strategies they use to survive.

Ecology

Bugs in the News!

http://people.ku.edu/~jbrown/bugs.html

Bugs in the News! is not about insects but about viruses, bacteria, and other microorganisms such as E. coli. E. coli is a helpful bacterium when it is in our large intestines: It helps us digest food. However, when it contaminates meat or local water supplies and enters our stomachs, E. coli causes health problems.

Digital Learning Center for Microbial Ecology

http://commtechlab.msu.edu/sites/dlc-me/

Learn about the "Microbe of the Month" featured at this site. Visit the Microbe Zoo, with microbe-rich environments at "dirtland," "the snack bar," and other buggy spots.

Dragonfly Trees Activities

http://www.units.muohio.edu/dragonfly/trees.HTMLX

Here you can learn about trees by engaging in different activities. Topics include tree shapes, seeds, and how trees protect their space.

Fun Facts About Fungi

http://herbarium.usu.edu/fungi/FunFacts/factindx.htm

This catalog explains about fungi: what they are, where they are found, of what use they are to people. You can make a collection and presentation on fungi, enhanced by this site. Look for fungi in shady, moist areas, especially following rainy periods. Put them on display in sealed containers and describe how they grow. Did you find them in a grassy area? On the bark of a rotting tree? Under a rock overhang?

Illusions and Perception

Grand Illusions

http://www.grand-illusions.com/

Hall of Illusions

http://psylux.psych.tu-dresden.de/i1/kaw/diverses%20
Material/www.illusionworks.com/index.html

Sandlot Science

http://www.sandlotscience.com/

Seeing More Than Your Eye Does

http://serendip.brynmawr.edu/bb/blindspot1.html

If you are interested in blind spots and optical illusions, visit these Web sites and try the experiments there. You will learn about how the eye perceives shapes and colors and how it delivers information to the brain through the optic nerve. You can compare different people's reactions to optical illusions. Do certain people experience them more than others? Is visual perception related to age or gender?

Human Anatomy

The Heart: An Online Exploration

http://sln.fi.edu/biosci/biosci.html

At this Web site you can study the structure of the human heart. You can wander around vessels as if you were a blood cell. Learn how people discovered things about the heart through past research.

Human Anatomy Online

http://www.innerbody.com/

This site is a fun, interactive collection of illustrations of the human body with animations and thousands of descriptive links. Human Anatomy Online uses Java applets to show images and select anatomy parts. You can focus on one particular anatomical system, such as the skeletal system, the nervous system, or the reproductive system.

Neuroscience for Kids
http://faculty.washington.edu/chudler/neurok.html
This home page has been created for elementary- and secondary-school students and teachers who would like to learn more about the nervous system. It contains activities and experiments relating to the brain and spinal cord.

The Visible Human Project
http://www.madsci.org/~lynn/VH/
In the Visible Human Project, scientists took slices of frozen human tissue and made eighteen thousand images. At this site, you can view the images in great detail from actual photos and videos. This project will help you understand a three-dimensional picture of the human body, inside and out.

Chapter 4

Earth Science Projects Using the Internet

Caroline wanted to do her earth science project on the earth's interior. She lives in the West Coast city of San Francisco, where there are many minor earthquakes and sometimes large ones. The earthquakes made her curious about the structure of the earth. What is inside it? What would you find if you kept digging? How does the earth change over time? Why do certain areas of the world have more earthquakes than others?

Although Caroline did not remember it, she was a baby in the 1989 earthquake in Loma Prieta, California. It was the first major event on the San Andreas fault since the infamous earthquake of 1906. She learned this and more at the following sites:

UC Berkeley Seismological Laboratory

http://www.seismo.berkeley.edu/seismo/faq/1989_0.html

USGS Earthquake Hazards Program, Northern California

http://quake.wr.usgs.gov/

Caroline wanted to compare this earthquake to an earthquake in New York to see why quakes are so violent in the region in which she lives. She looked up the New York earthquake nearest in time to the Loma Prieta quake at these sites:

Lamont-Doherty Cooperative Seismographic Network (LCSN)

http://www.ldeo.columbia.edu/LCSN/

Weston Observatory at Boston College

http://www.bc.edu/research/westonobservatory/

In 1985 an earthquake in Newburgh, New York, registered 4.0 on the Richter scale. The Richter scale is a measure of earthquake intensity. The higher the number, the more violent the earthquake. The Newburgh earthquake was a significant event, but nothing like the 7.1-magnitude quake of Loma Prieta.

Caroline continued her research to learn more about the forces that shape the earth. She visited these sites:

This Dynamic Earth

http://pubs.usgs.gov/publications/text/dynamic.html

Earth's Interior & Plate Tectonics

http://www.solarviews.com/eng/earthint.htm

The Franklin Institute Science Museum: Earthforce

http://sln.fi.edu/earth/earth.html

The first and second sites showed cross sections of the earth and explained what is inside it. Caroline learned that the earth has a nickel-iron core surrounded by the mantle and then the crust. Different regions within these layers have their own names and properties. She also learned about the boundaries of ocean plates. Portions of the earth's crust, called plates, slide around. This causes earthquakes at the boundaries and has led to the position and shape of our modern continents.

Caroline began to form a hypothesis, that earthquakes occur in regions where one plate meets another. The rubbing of plates against each other, pushing and pulling, could be the source of earthquake energy. Perhaps California has more numerous and energetic earthquakes than New York, she theorized, because it is closer to the edge of a plate.

The third site was an online exhibit provided by the Franklin Institute Science Museum. It explained earth forces in the plates and at the ocean bottom. It also described tsunamis, which are giant waves that result from earthquakes. Tsunamis have killed many people throughout history. In December 2004, one tsunami in the Indian Ocean killed over two hundred thousand people.

Coastal & Marine Geology Program

http://marine.usgs.gov/

Western Coastal & Marine Geology

http://walrus.wr.usgs.gov/

At these sites, Caroline learned more about the ocean in particular. They explained how scientists study the ocean floor.

Marine geologists describe how the earth got its present geography. They also work on more practical problems: where to look for minerals, oil, and other resources.

MTU Volcanoes Page

http://www.geo.mtu.edu/volcanoes/

On this page, the Michigan Technological University shares its information about volcanoes. It describes, with maps, where volcanoes are found and how scientists study them. It provides links to many other institutions that study volcanoes.

From these various sites, Caroline learned that San Francisco is located at the boundary of the Pacific plate. Indeed, the entire West Coast of the United States is an area active with volcanoes and earthquakes. A mountain range—the Rockies—extends from Canada to Mexico. New York, on the other hand, is not at the edge of a crustal plate. Its smaller mountains are much older and have eroded over time. No active volcanoes are in the state.

Caroline wanted to show how the earth's plates move. She wanted to communicate the type of processes that have determined the earth's geologic history. If she could model the movement of the earth's plates, she could show how the plates generate heat. She could also show how such activity results in earthquakes and volcanoes, and how these cause the earth to change over time.

Geologists believe that the continents once formed a large landmass called Pangaea. Pangaea broke apart, and the pieces slid over the earth's fluid interior to form today's continents. Caroline made an exhibit for her science project to demonstrate this. She went to the site Earth's Interior & Plate Tectonics (above) and dragged the Crustal Plate Boundaries file to the desktop of her computer. She opened this new "plates.gif" file in a paint program and enlarged it by 400 percent. She printed out the image and pasted it on thick cardboard. Then she cut the continents out, mounted magnets on the back of them, and put them in an iron tray. Visitors to her exhibit could move the continents together, like pieces of a puzzle, to form Pangaea. Then they could pull them apart to their modern positions.

Caroline also visited

University of North Dakota's Volcano World

http://volcano.und.edu/

to look for ways to build models of a volcano. Within this site, Caroline found a page entirely devoted to the topic:

Building Volcano Models

http://volcano.und.nodak.edu/vwdocs/volc_models/models.html

This page had a variety of different ways to construct models, using materials such as clay, cardboard, and papier-mâché. Caroline decided that building a model in three dimensions would help people understand the structure (shape) and activity in a volcano.

Since Caroline got images and ideas from these Web sites, she made sure to cite them in her references. Her citations looked like this:

Scott Rowland, "How Long Does It Take for Magma To Cool So You Can Walk On It?" (no date specified). Available Online: http://volcano.und.nodak.edu/vwdocs/frequent_questions/grp1/question46.html [April 2, 2005].

University of North Dakota, *Volcano World:* "Simple Clay Models," (no date specified). Available online: http://volcano.und.nodak.edu/vwdocs/volc_models/clay.html [April 2, 2005].

Where possible, she cited the author, name of Web page, original publication date, address, and date she visited. Sometimes it is hard to figure out all this information from Web sites. Not all information is always present. Caroline did the best she could to document her sources.

Finally, Caroline was confused about the difference between S and P waves in earthquakes. She found someone to answer her questions at this site:

Ask-A-Geologist

http://walrus.wr.usgs.gov/ask-a-geologist/

She e-mailed her question to an actual U.S. Geological Survey earth scientist and received an answer within a few days.

With all the information she had gathered, Caroline was able to show clearly that regions of earth activity occur at plate boundaries. Earthquakes, volcanoes, and plate edges are clustered in the same places around the world. Areas between plate boundaries have much less seismic and volcanic activity.

Other Sites to Help You in Your Earth Science Research

Advanced Earthquake Sites

Seismosurfing the Internet for Earthquake Data

http://www.geophys.washington.edu/seismosurfing.html

Use this site as a home base to gather and analyze earthquake data. Who knows, maybe you can predict the next major earthquake!

Virtual Courseware: Earthquake

http://vearthquake.calstatela.edu/eec/Earthquake/

The Virtual Earthquake site is good for advanced high school students. It allows you to find the epicenter of a mythical earthquake. When an earthquake occurs, the ground moves, and this causes vibrations and sound waves that travel through the earth. These waves move outward from the center of the earthquake and travel away. The more time that passes, the farther they travel, like waves in the ocean. Seismologists use science and math to figure out the starting point of the vibrations.

Earth Science and Geology Sites

Careers in Geoscience

http://www.science.uwaterloo.ca/earth/geoscience/careers.html

At this site you can find out how people become geoscientists. Who are today's geoscientists? What do they do? What can a person do with this training? The site answers these and other career questions.

Earth Sciences

Science@NASA

http://science.hq.nasa.gov/

This government site features puzzles, games, research, and press releases related to earth science.

Map-It: Form-Based Simple Map Generator

http://stellwagen.er.usgs.gov/mapit/

This site lets you enter longitude and latitude values. Then you click on a button to get a Mercator projection map of the region you indicated.

U.S. Geological Survey Learning Web
http://education.usgs.gov/
This is the USGS education site, with plenty of resources for students. It teaches about glacier movement, seafloor spreading, arctic delta formation, landslides, and fossil formation. It also explains mapmaking processes.

USGS Radon in Earth, Air, and Water
http://energy.cr.usgs.gov/radon/radonhome.html
This site tells you about radon, a noble gas that can be a health hazard in homes. You can learn about where radon is located and how it is measured. Is your home or community at risk for radon poisoning?

Earth History

American Museum of Natural History: Resources for Learning
http://www.amnh.org/education/resources
Click on Earth Science for abundant science topics relating to land, water, and air.

Natural History Museum of London, Department of Palaeontology
http://www.nhm.ac.uk/palaeontology/

Paleontological Research Institution
http://www.priweb.org/

Royal Tyrrell Museum

http://www.tyrrellmuseum.com/

University of California Museum of Paleontology

http://www.ucmp.berkeley.edu/index.html

> *These sites describe the history of the earth. They share information about plants, animals, and geologic events. They also display fossils, teaching about the evolution of species and earth's changing geology.*

Earth Imaging Systems

GOES Project Science

http://goes.gsfc.nasa.gov/

Jet Propulsion Laboratory: Earth

http://www.jpl.nasa.gov/earth/

National Geophysical Data Center

http://www.ngdc.noaa.gov/ngdc.html

Ocean Surface Topography from Space

http://topex-www.jpl.nasa.gov/

> *Learn how scientists use satellites and radar to understand climate and weather. They use imaging instruments to collect data about the ocean floor, wildfires, the climate, earthquakes, sea level changes, and other topics. You can download images, data, and video clips from the Web to do your own research.*

Minerals and Other Natural Resources

Mineral Exhibits

http://www.geology.wisc.edu/~museum/old/minerals.html

This University of Wisconsin site lists common minerals, many of which you can find near your home. You can collect, identify, and classify minerals. (Many science stores such as the Discovery Channel Store and the Nature Company sell hard-to-find specimens.) This site has an especially good exhibit on fluorescent rocks and minerals, which glow under ultraviolet light. Your teacher may be able to provide you with fluorescent mineral samples and a mineral light.

National Museum of Natural History, Department of Mineral Sciences

http://www.minerals.si.edu/

Smithsonian Gem & Mineral Collection

http://www.gimizu.de/sgmcol/

These sites have images of minerals you might not find near your home.

Virtual Cave

http://www.goodearthgraphics.com/virtcave.html

Are you a spelunker? At this site you can view good-quality photographs of different mineral samples gathered from caves all around the world.

Paleontology and Fossil Records

Classroom of the Future: Earth Science Explorer

http://www.cotf.edu/ete/modules/msese/explorer.html

You can learn about earth systems and dinosaurs. This site explores some of the theories of why the dinosaurs might have become extinct so suddenly. One theory is that a giant asteroid crashed into the earth. Following the explosive impact, huge amounts of water and ash went into the atmosphere, blocking the sun and cooling the climate for years.

Skeletons
http://www.units.muohio.edu/dragonfly/skeletons/index.htmlx

This site has a simple explanation of how fossils form. It leads to a "virtual dinosaur dig," where you pick the tools and strategies for finding ancient reptilian remains.

What Is a Fossil and How Is It Preserved?
http://www.pa.msu.edu/~sciencet/ask_st/082097.html

This scientist's answer to the question tells about the different types of fossil formations. Fossils can be formed by preservation, mineral preservation, casts, or imprints (such as footprints).

Volcano-Related Web Sites

If volcanoes interest you, there are many Web sites you can visit.

Cascades Volcano Observatory
http://vulcan.wr.usgs.gov/home.html

This Web site describes volcanoes in the Pacific Northwest. It has many maps and other graphic images you can use. You could build a working model of an instrument used by seismologists or volcanologists. This would be useful for a project on human safety. If you live near an active volcano, you could create a volcanic eruption detection plan and emergency evacuation plan.

Dante II: Volcano Explorer

http://volcano.und.nodak.edu/vwdocs/vw_news/dante.html

When scientists want to study an active volcano that is too dangerous for humans to enter, they can send in a robot: Dante II. Dante bravely ventured into Alaska's Mt. Spurr to get readings of gas fumes. This technology has uses in areas other than volcano research. Robots like Dante can be used to clean up hazardous waste sites or to diffuse bombs.

NASA EOS IDS Volcanology Team

http://eos.higp.hawaii.edu//

The National Aeronautics and Space Administration (NASA) helps volcanologists by using a technology called remote sensing. This site explains how the process is done. It shares information discovered by government-funded research.

University of North Dakota: Volcano World

http://volcano.und.nodak.edu/

This Web site features a volcano of the week. You can find out which volcanoes are erupting where. You can view images and videos of volcanoes in action.

Volcano Watch

http://hvo.wr.usgs.gov/volcanowatch/

This weekly newsletter comes from volcano country: Hawaii. It focuses on the volcanoes of Hawaii and gives updates on their activity. Produced by scientists at the U.S. Geological Survey's Hawaiian Volcano Observatory, it contains a library of articles with a search engine.

Weather

In Chapter 1, we looked at how Kimberly used several weather sites to prepare her project. Here are some other weather-related sites:

El Niño: Hot Air Over Hot Water

http://sln.fi.edu/weather/nino/nino.html

El Niño is a huge patch of warm Pacific water that affects the climate in North America. At this site, the Franklin Institute Science Museum explains what El Niño is. There are activities you can do to demonstrate the thermal processes at work.

Hurricane

http://www.miamisci.org/hurricane/

Southern Florida is a region that gets hit with many hurricanes. This site, from the Miami Museum of Science, describes the inside of a hurricane. You can learn about the instruments meteorologists use to make physical measurements during these violent storms. Family members share their frightening stories from actual storms.

Ice & Snow

http://www.units.muohio.edu/dragonfly/snow/

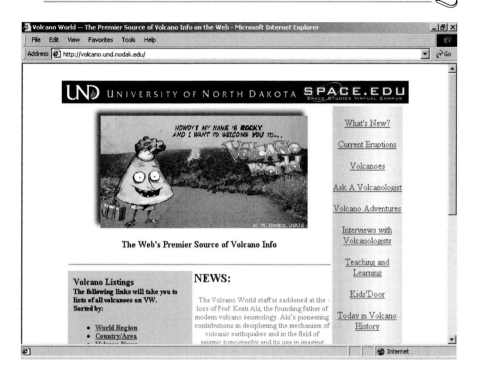

Volcano information can be found at the Volcano World site.

You can virtually visit Antarctica, learn about snow and ice, and experiment with snowflakes.

National Weather Service

http://www.nws.noaa.gov/

The National Weather Service is a government organization in charge of warning people about coming weather events. It provides information to weather bureaus at newspapers and at television and radio stations. This helps people prepare for blizzards, heat waves, and other storms and important meteorological events.

National Weather Service Climate Prediction Center

http://www.cpc.ncep.noaa.gov/

This is another online resource for El Niño and other weather events. At the Climate Prediction Center, you can get pictures that contain temperature, wind, and precipitation data resulting from El Niño. This page also has a "U.S. Hazards Assessment" section that predicts bad weather.

Chapter 5

Environmental Science Projects Using the Internet

Hydrology is the study of water in its various forms. Water can be a liquid, solid, or gas (vapor). It can be fresh or contain salt and other minerals. It can be clean or polluted. Every known life form uses water to survive. Humans rely on the fresh, clean version of this precious commodity. Less than one percent of water on Earth is available as fresh and unfrozen. As the human population grows and reaches the remotest areas of our globe, we have to protect this natural resource ever more carefully.

Manny's school was preparing for its annual science fair. Manny wanted to enter a project in the seventh-grade life sciences category. He lived on a farm with a pond and a stream and decided it would be perfect if he could do a project on the hydrology of his home environment. He knew that these water bodies were not as healthy as they once had been: His father told him the water used to be clearer and the fishing used to be better. Manny was interested in finding out what was harming the ecology and what could be done about it. He had heard something about eutrophication and low oxygen levels.

Manny got Web site recommendations from various sources. He tried a Web search on his own for "water," "hydrology," "stream," and other terms. As it turned out, there is an entire section of Yahoo! devoted to hydrology:

Yahoo!: Hydrology
http://dir.yahoo.com/Science/earth_sciences/hydrology/index.
html

> *This area of Yahoo! led Manny to many water-related sites.*

Manny then asked his teacher if she knew of any hydrology sites. She showed him a magazine article that had environmental education Web site reviews. He visited this site first:

Ocean Planet
http://seawifs.gsfc.nasa.gov/ocean_planet.html

> *The Smithsonian's Ocean Planet site gave Manny lots of information about the types of water quality measurements scientists take. Manny started to understand the earth's water cycle, which was valuable background information for his project.*

He then checked:

USGS: Water Resources of the United States
http://water.usgs.gov/

This site has real-time data, meaning that it has actual statistics for present water conditions. It also has historical data and links to other water-related sites. However, Manny was most excited about something else the site offered: free posters. He wrote to the U.S. Geological Survey (USGS), and they sent him posters on wetlands, water use, groundwater, wastewater, and water quality.

Manny did a formal study of the bodies of water on his farm. He got a test kit for measuring oxygen. With his teacher's help, he was able to measure the oxygen in the water and compare it to the oxygen levels in more balanced bodies of water. He found that oxygen, a life-sustaining gas, was indeed low in the water on his farm. He also monitored temperature, depth, and velocity. He studied the wildlife, observing the fish, mammals, amphibians, and plant life in the stream and pond. This was the part of the project where he really supported his hypothesis—that fertilizer was getting into the water, causing algae to grow and use up all the oxygen and nutrients needed by plants and fish.

For the final part of his project, Manny made environmental recommendations for the protection and preservation of the hydrologic environment on his farm. The following site was useful for this part of his research:

National Marine Fisheries Service
http://www.nmfs.noaa.gov/
This governmental Web site contained links to actual written passages from the Endangered Species Act.

Manny concluded that his farm, and neighboring farms, could make some operating changes that would improve the health of the stream. He suggested that a change in the type of fertilizer used and the way it was applied might help restore the ecological balance of the water. By making some simple modifications in their techniques, the farmers might be able to reduce their effects on aquatic life. Manny shared his recommendations with his father and with neighboring farmers.

Other Sites to Help You in Your Environmental Science Research

Advanced Hydrology Sites

These sites are more advanced water information sources. Your teacher may have ideas on how you can use the government-funded data available here.

Global Hydrology Resource Center

http://ghrc.msfc.nasa.gov/

This is a data-rich site with measurements on wind speed, water vapor, and other hydrology-related quantities.

National Snow and Ice Data Center

http://www-nsidc.colorado.edu/

This site provides data on snow and ice in digital form. It has an education section with questions and answers on ice and snow, glaciers, and avalanche awareness. It also contains a "mapping and gridding primer," which teaches about mapping. It defines such terms as points, pixels, grids, *and* cells. *You can learn about how satellites are used to create maps.*

Oak Ridge National Laboratory Distributed Active Archive Center

http://www-eosdis.ornl.gov/

This site provides remote-sensing biogeochemical data on wetlands, grasslands, and water bodies.

Ecological Environments

The World Wide Web brings places to you that you might not otherwise get to see. At the following sites, you can study remote ecological environments from home and school.

Desert USA

http://www.desertusa.com/life.html

Rainforest Action Network

http://www.ran.org/

At this site you can learn about rain forests and find out how to help preserve these valuable areas of our environment.

Tropical Rainforest In Suriname

http://www.ecocam.com/nature/Suriname.html

Virtual Antarctica

http://www.doc.ic.ac.uk/~kpt/terraquest/va/

Virtual Tour: Antarctica

http://astro.uchicago.edu/cara/vtour/

These well-crafted sites examine particular places on our planet. You can study different environments at each. The sites describe climate, plants and animals (flora and fauna), food sources, human culture, and conservation.

Many Internet sites describe different environments. The Virtual Tour: Antarctica site details the animals and plants of Antarctica.

The Franklin Institute: Water In The City

http://www.fi.edu/city/water/

> *You do not have to live on a farm to care or learn about water. "Water in the City" explains urban water supplies.*

Learn about reservoirs, sewers, water quality, and more, and then try a few of the water activities posted there.

Webs of Life

http://www.units.muohio.edu/dragonfly/webs/

At this site you can explore the islands of Baja and learn about the ecological niche of spiders. "Backyard Islands" will lead you to learning about your own home environment.

Global Forums and Projects

Alaska Science Forum

http://www.gi.alaska.edu/ScienceForum/index.html

Do you have a yearning to visit Alaska? This Web page is provided as a public service by the Geophysical Institute, University of Alaska Fairbanks. It leads you to Alaska-related resources in every science you can think of, from agriculture to zoology. Visit the science forum or find out how the 2004 earthquake in Sumatra was felt all the way in Alaska.

The Jason Project

http://www.jasonproject.org/

Every year, the Jason Foundation for Education sponsors a scientific expedition. Using advanced telecommunications, students can take part in live, interactive programs following the expedition. A recent Jason expedition took students and teachers on a virtual tour of Mars. Visit this Web site if you think you might want to become involved with the Jason Project with your teacher and class.

LEO-15 Ocean Research Station

http://marine.rutgers.edu/nurp/facilities.html

LEO-15 is an underwater long-term ecological laboratory. This Web site provides middle-school-level Internet activities in ecology. You can visit this site to study coastal upwelling on the New Jersey shore. You can also study the Gulf Stream and phytoplankton (microscopic sea plants).

One Sky, Many Voices

http://onesky.engin.umich.edu/

This site has four-week and eight-week environmental science programs that use the Internet and other technological communications tools. Different projects are featured all the time. If the timing is right, you might join one for your project. Global science topics are featured here.

U.S. Environmental Protection Agency

http://www.epa.gov/

No chapter on environmental science would be complete without mentioning the U.S. Environmental Protection Agency. This federal organization is devoted to safeguarding our natural resources. Its home page has links for students, including very specific activities you can try at home and school. Start here, or jump directly to this next site:

U.S. EPA Kid's Page

http://www.epa.gov/kids/

where you will find activities on water quality and experiments on water filtration.

Other Environmental Science Sites

Demographic Data Viewer Home Page

http://plue.sedac.ciesin.org/plue/ddviewer/ddv30-USMEX/

This is a mapmaking Web site that you can use whether or not your Web browser has Java. At this site, you can generate maps showing United States census information such as age, gender, income, race, and housing information. You can generate different maps of where you live to help show the environmental impact that population growth has on your community.

Indoor and Outdoor Air Pollution

http://www.lbl.gov/Education/ELSI/pollution-main.html

This government site teaches about sources and effects of air pollution. You can use it as a basis for a study of pollution where you live. For instance, you can place clear tape in various locations, sticky side exposed, for three days and then count, through a microscope, the number of particles that adhere per square centimeter. How do the levels of air pollution compare between an area around a streetlamp and one in your bedroom? (Hopefully they are less inside!)

Satellite Photographs and Imaging

USGS Terraweb for Kids

http://terraweb.wr.usgs.gov/TRS/kids/

This is a directory of links related to satellite imaging and views of earth from space.

Chapter 6

Astronomy Projects Using the Internet

Keira wanted to do an astronomy project for her fifth-grade science class. She had a telescope on her back porch that she used to view the night sky. At certain times of the year, she could see planets such as Venus and Mars. Planets orbit the sun, which is called their revolution. They also spin about their axes, which is called their rotation. For her project, Keira decided to compare the rotation and revolution of different planets to determine whether these properties might have an effect on the formation of life. Earth is the only planet that we know with certainty has life on it. It is one of the terrestrial planets. Venus and Mars are also terrestrial. They are similar to Earth in size. They were apparently formed in the same way as Earth, by the gathering of clumps of matter. And they contain similar elements. Keira hypothesized that some planets have conditions that would prevent the formation of advanced life, but that Earth conditions, including rotation and revolution rates, support life.

Keira started her online research at

NASA Home Page

http://www.nasa.gov/

The National Aeronautics and Space Administration is a large federal agency devoted to space exploration. Keira found a "Search the NASA Web" link, clicked there, and entered keywords such as "rotation" and "revolution." Many links came up. She learned about the planets by visiting these sites and reading the information and viewing the images found there.

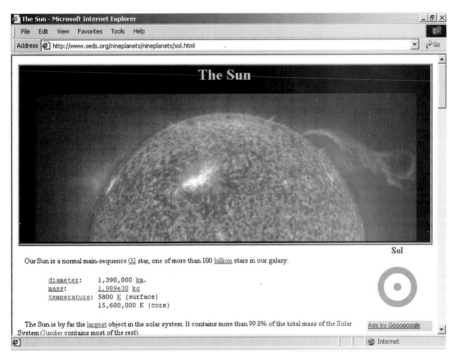

Facts about the solar system, as well as images, can be found at the many different planet Web sites.

Keira began to learn about the different features of planets and the ways scientists measure them. She used some additional planetary study sites in her project, including the following:

NASA Space Place

http://spaceplace.nasa.gov/en/kids/

Here she found space-related projects, animations, facts, and games.

The Nine Planets

http://www.seds.org/nineplanets/nineplanets/

Welcome to the Planets

http://pds.jpl.nasa.gov/planets/

These two sites provide good introductory information on the planets.

Keira was able to click on links for each planet to get pictures and data. She used Microsoft Word to make a table summarizing data she found on the Web. The purpose was to compare the planets. Here are the first few rows of her table:

PLANET	ORBIT RADIUS (AU)	PERIOD OF ROTATION (Days)	PERIOD OF REVOLUTION (Years)
Mercury	0.387	59.0	0.241
Venus	0.723	243	0.615
Earth	1.00	1.00	1.00

Already Keira was starting to get a picture of how the planets differ. Mercury is only a third the distance from the sun as Earth. It would be much too hot for life as we know it to exist there. She realized Venus, too, would be a poor place for life because of its long day. This long day, combined with a carbon dioxide atmosphere, would make the surface of Venus extremely hot. She concluded that a planet much different from Earth in its rotation and revolution would be unlikely to produce life similar to ours.

Keira wanted some images of the planets from outer space and at their surfaces. She found them at these sites:

Planetary Image Finders

http://ic.arc.nasa.gov/ic/projects/bayes-group/Atlas/

Views of the Solar System

http://www.solarviews.com/eng/homepage.htm

She discovered that there were thousands of images of planets on the Internet, and more and more were made available each day. She did not want to use too many images in her project, so she selected three from outer space and three close-ups of the surfaces. She printed them out in color to include in her report. She decided it would be best to go with a few large, detailed images rather than too many smaller ones.

Keira wanted to show the motion of the planets around the sun, so she used this online simulation:

Planetary Orbit Simulators

http://www.ifigure.com/science/astro/astro.htm

Keira was able to view moving images of planet paths in controlled simulations. This inspired her to observe the planets themselves from her home. She used her telescope to try to locate them. She got information from the Skywatch column in her local newspaper on where and when to look. Her own observations were an important part of her report.

Other Sites to Help You in Your Astronomy Research

Advanced Astronomy Sites

The Hopkins Ultraviolet Telescope Project
http://praxis.pha.jhu.edu/hut.html

University of California Observatories
http://www.ucolick.org/

> *These are advanced telescope sites. Astronomers use different types of telescopes in their studies. The first telescopes were optical telescopes. Now they also rely on radio, infrared, and ultraviolet telescopes.*

Additional telescope Web sites are listed at these two directories:

Radio Telescope Resources
http://www.stsci.edu/astroweb/cat-radio.html

Yahoo: Science: Astronomy: Telescopes
http://www.yahoo.com/Science/Astronomy/Telescopes/

> *These sites lead to telescope Web sites around the world.*

Aurora Borealis

The Aurora Page

http://www.geo.mtu.edu/weather/aurora/

The aurora borealis, also known as the northern lights, is one of the most beautiful celestial events you can witness. Normally it is difficult to see the northern lights unless you live very far north, such as in Alaska. But on Michigan Tech's Aurora Page, you can read the latest sighting reports for North America, the latest three-day forecast, and the latest three-hour reports.

Auroras: Paintings in the Sky

http://www.exploratorium.edu/learning_studio/auroras/index.html

Here is another site where you can find out how auroras are formed and why they have such brilliant colors.

Comets and Other Astronomical Objects

Discovery Is NEAR

http://near.jhuapl.edu/

This is the home page for the NEAR project, which examines asteroids and other chunks of matter orbiting the sun in the neighborhood of Earth. Such studies shed light on Earth's history: how Earth and the other planets were formed; when Earth was struck by asteroids; and how life might have formed.

Small Planet Communications

http://www.smplanet.com/science/SL9.html

This site describes how you can investigate Comet Shoemaker-Levy 9, which smashed into the planet Jupiter in July 1994. It gives instructions on how to create your own Web page of research findings. For your project, you can gather astronomical data from the Internet and create an informative Web site. You will have your own place on the information highway.

General Astronomy Resources

CNN Science and Space

http://www.cnn.com/TECH/space/

Here you will find breaking news on celestial events such as meteor showers and eclipses, NASA press releases, and other current stories.

Earth & Sky Radio Series Online

http://www.earthsky.com/

This site is devoted to the Earth & Sky Radio Series, which is all about astronomy, earth science, and environmental science. It has questions and answers, along with a searchable database. You can join the Earth & Sky mailing list at this site.

Goddard Space Flight Center: Astronomy Resource Center

http://heasarc.gsfc.nasa.gov/docs/outreach.html

This site is provided by NASA's High Energy Astrophysics Science Archive Research Center (HEASARC). It is the gateway to Imagine the Universe!, StarChild, Ask a NASA Scientist, and other space Web sites for students.

Jet Propulsion Laboratory
http://www.jpl.nasa.gov/

> *This government site is devoted to exploration of our solar system through the use of rocketry. It describes current and past missions through news stories and multimedia resources. Kids', Education, and Research sections have information of interest to students at all levels. Under "Missions," get the latest news and images collected from space!*

Observatorium
http://observe.arc.nasa.gov/nasa/core/shtml.html

> *Here, NASA's Observatorium posts Earth and space data for the public. The site has pictures of the planets and stars, and tells how those images were obtained.*

Windows to the Universe
http://www.windows.ucar.edu/

> *This project is funded by NASA. You can enter the Web site in a variety of ways—including using a CD-ROM or just a Web browser.*

Mars

The Daily Martian Weather Report
http://nova.stanford.edu/projects/mgs/dmwr.html

> *At this site you can study the temperature and weather on Mars in detail.*

Mars Exploration Program
http://mars.jpl.nasa.gov/

Mars Global Surveyor
http://mars.jpl.nasa.gov/mgs/

NASA Quest
http://questdb.arc.nasa.gov/content_search_space.htm

These sites include data and images brought to us by unmanned spaceflights to our red neighbor. Mars is so much like Earth in its properties that scientists debate whether life exists there or might have in the past.

The Moon and Lunar Landings

In the space race of the 1950s and '60s, the United States and the Soviet Union competed to be the first country to put a man on the moon. The Web is filled with moon resources that describe manned and unmanned missions to the moon and the features and properties of the moon itself.

Earth and Moon Viewer
http://www.fourmilab.ch/earthview/vplanet.html

This site has mapping functions that allow you to view Earth and the moon from different vantages in space using satellite imagery.

Lunar Exploration
http://nssdc.gsfc.nasa.gov/planetary/lunar/apollo_25th.html

This is a good starting point for moon research. It gives the historical background behind moon exploration and has links to all the major moon expeditions.

Moonlink
http://www.space-explorers.com/

In January 1998, Lunar Prospector *was launched to gather data about the moon's surface.* Space Explorers *is an Internet-based education program that uses data from NASA's Lunar Prospector mission.*

Project Apollo: Program Overview

http://science.ksc.nasa.gov/history/apollo/apollo.html

Here you will find information on the famous Apollo moon landings. This site has information about the crews, the launches, and the journeys. It links to other Apollo sites hosted by the government. Other sites that relate to the Apollo programs include:

The Apollo Program (1963–1972)

http://nssdc.gsfc.nasa.gov/planetary/lunar/apollo.html

Soviet Lunar Missions

http://nssdc.gsfc.nasa.gov/planetary/lunar/lunarussr.html

U.S. Centennial of Flight Commission: Project Apollo

http://www.centennialofflight.gov/essay/SPACEFLIGHT/apollo/SP19.htm

These sites offer historical background, technical details of the flights, and scientific findings.

Surveyor to the Moon (1966–1968)

http://nssdc.gsfc.nasa.gov/planetary/lunar/surveyor.html

Before sending people to the moon, we sent unmanned crafts to take pictures and determine whether a visit would be safe for astronauts. This site has experiment descriptions for Surveyor 1 *through* Surveyor 7.

Other Planets

3-D Tour of the Solar System

http://www.lpi.usra.edu/research/stereo_atlas/SS3D.HTM

Put on your 3-D glasses and see the surfaces of planets in three dimensions. Special photography techniques make stereo space images available. Ordering instructions are also provided for an inexpensive CD-ROM version of the site.

The Galileo Project

http://nssdc.gsfc.nasa.gov/planetary/galileo.html

The Galileo mission used the gravitational fields of Venus and Earth to send a spacecraft to Jupiter. When Galileo got there, it dropped a probe into the atmosphere of the huge gas planet. The probe sent information back to Earth. This Web site presents information from this mission.

Exploration NASA

http://www.nasa.gov/externalflash/Vision/index.html

This is the home page of NASA, a great place to begin studying about solar system exploration, manned and unmanned.

How Old Are You on Mercury?

http://library.thinkquest.org/CR0210901/age.htm

This short Thinkquest project shows you how to calculate your age on different planets, where the revolutions take a different length of time than our year on Earth.

A Solar System Scale Model Meta Page

http://www.vendian.org/mncharity/dir3/solarsystem/

This site deals exclusively with the size and proportion of the solar system. Visit it if you need to create models of planet size and distance to support your project. It is a directory of different sites devoted to making such models.

Space Travel

Mir Space Station

http://liftoff.msfc.nasa.gov/rsa/mir.html

Learn about Russia's space ventures. Research the history and design of the Mir space station.

NASA: Human Space Flight

http://spaceflight.nasa.gov/home/index.html

At this site you can chart the progress of current space missions. Find out about the crews and their planned activities. This site offers sneak previews of coming trips.

Stars and Nebulae

The Constellations and Their Stars

http://www.astro.wisc.edu/~dolan/constellations/constellations.html

This Web site teaches about the constellations. Constellations are groups of stars that we see from Earth's surface. The stars are related mostly by the way they appear: Our ancestors looked up in the night sky and saw shapes of animals and people. This site presents a

combination of historical information, maps, and scientific information.

Google Sky Maps and Atlases

http://directory.google.com/Top/Science/Astronomy/
Amateur/Sky_Maps_and_Atlases/

Many Web sites allow you to simulate the night sky with interactive star maps. You pick a location, time, and view, and the computer shows what you would see in real life. In some maps you can choose to show such features as constellations and meteor showers.

National Geographic Star Journey

http://www.nationalgeographic.com/features/97/stars/

At this site you can view a star map of the night sky. You can move around the night sky and zoom in on particular regions. You will also be able to see images from the Hubble Space Telescope by clicking on them within the map.

StarChild

http://starchild.gsfc.nasa.gov/docs/StarChild/StarChild.html

Stars have properties just like planets. They have size, mass, color, and other measurable features. StarChild is a learning center for young astronomers. It is a good source of information on stars for students just entering middle school, and it has a glossary of space-related terms.

Star Colors and Temperatures

http://zebu.uoregon.edu/~soper/Stars/color.html

This Web page explains why stars have different colors. Different temperatures, in part, account for the stars' appearance.

The Web Nebulae

http://astro.nineplanets.org/twn/

Nebulae are clouds of dust and gas that, when viewed through telescopes, are often colorful and beautiful. This site has a collection of pleasing images of nebulae.

The Sun

The 150-Foot Solar Tower at Mt. Wilson Observatory

http://www.astro.ucla.edu/~obs/intro.html

The telescope at California's Mt. Wilson Observatory is aimed at the sun. You would not want to view the sun directly, since the sun can damage your eyes. At Mt. Wilson, scientists observe the sun indirectly, using special optical and photographic techniques. Here you can view images from the observatory and find out about sun spots and magnetic activity.

Stanford Solar Center

http://solar-center.stanford.edu/

At the Stanford Solar Center, you can learn about eclipses and view eclipse images. This Web site has fun activities such as making a spectroscope or a sundial.

Virtual Sun

http://www.michielb.nl/sun/kaft.htm

This Web site offers a twenty-minute virtual tour of the sun, complete with movies.

The Hubble Site

http://hubblesite.org/

What is the big deal about the Hubble Space Telescope? It is simple: Since it is located in outer space, above Earth's atmosphere, there is no atmosphere or clouds to distort the images that it collects. This provides crystal clear images not possible from Earth. This site contains Hubble images and tells how they were gathered.

Chapter 7

Chemistry Projects Using the Internet

Dylan had become very interested in acids and bases. He had learned how to use litmus and pH paper to test the acidity of chemicals. He knew from science class that many substances at home are acids and bases. Vinegar and lemon juice are common household acids. Baking soda is a base. Water is neutral. Dylan decided to do a more formal study of household acids and bases. He wanted to know: Which substances are acids, which are bases, and which are neutral? Are there any patterns to be found in the chemicals at home?

To prepare for his project, he did a search for "acids and bases" at this student site:

Chem4Kids!

http://www.chem4kids.com/

This Web page came up:

Chem4Kids Acids & Bases

http://www.chem4kids.com/files/react_acidbase.html

It described the pH scale for measuring acidity. This scale ranges from 0 (acidic) to 14 (basic), with 7 being neutral. It gave examples of acids and bases and their actual pH values. It defined important acid-base terms and explained the chemistry of acid-base reactions—all in simple terms. Another useful site he found was:

The pH Factor

http://www.miamisci.org/ph/default.html

This site had interesting information on tasting nontoxic acids and bases. Acids taste sour, and bases taste bitter. Following

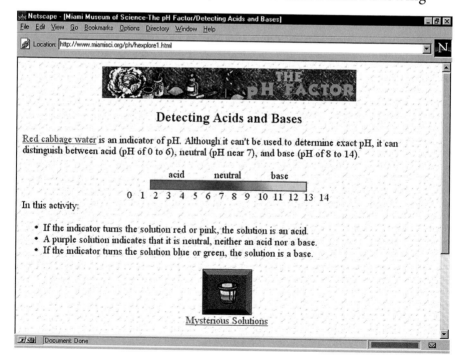

The pH scale for measuring acids and bases can be used for your science project.

the instructions there, Dylan was able to verify this with his tongue using small quantities of safe-to-taste chemicals such as citrus juices, baking soda, and antacid.

In the main part of his research, Dylan measured the pH of different household substances using pH paper he got from his teacher. (He did NOT taste these.) He made a table of his data. Here are some of his findings:

SUBSTANCE	pH	CLASSIFICATION
lemonade	4	acid
apple juice	5	acid
egg white	8	base
milk	8	base
toilet bowl cleaner with bleach	1	strong acid
window cleaner	10	base
laundry detergent	9	base
ammonia	13	strong base
water	7	neutral
furniture polish	7	neutral
corn oil	7	neutral
cola	5	acid
stomach antacid	8	base

From the results of his experiment, Dylan formed some important conclusions. Citrus juices and soft drinks are acidic. Oils and water are neutral. Cleansers and antacids are basic. Sometimes there were exceptions to these trends. Toilet bowl cleaner turned out to be acidic. He found hydrochloric acid in the list of ingredients, which explained this anomaly. In fact, many of the substances he studied had ingredients written on the packages. Citric acid, ammonium hydroxide, and acetic acid are examples of chemicals that he found influence the pH of many home products.

Dylan took his research one step further to find out what makes something an acid or a base. Some useful definitions he found on the Web sites above were:

Acids: Chemicals that donate a hydrogen ion, or H^+, when they react.

Bases: Chemicals that donate a hydroxide ion, or OH^- when they react.

Hydrogen and oxygen are very important elements in chemistry. To learn more about these elements in particular, he visited a periodic table on the Web:

WebElements

http://www.webelements.com/

WebElements had a virtual periodic table of the elements. Dylan clicked his mouse on hydrogen to find out about this element. He learned its atomic weight, atomic number, and physical properties. He also learned its chemical importance and some historical information about it.

Other Sites to Help You in Your Chemistry Research

Chemicals

K–12 Water and Ice Module

http://www.edinformatics.com/math_science/water_ice.htm

This site contains information about water and ice. You will find laboratory simulations, molecular simulations, and concepts and challenges.

Science Is Fun in the Lab of Shakhashiri

http://scifun.chem.wisc.edu/scifun.html

Chemistry professor Bassam Z. Shakhashiri, at the University of Wisconsin–Madison, is the master of chemical demonstrations. He reveals his secrets at this site. One section contains chemical experiments you can do at home.

What You Always Wanted to Know About Salt

http://www.saltinstitute.org/4.html

This site has information on one of the most famous chemicals of all: sodium chloride, otherwise known as table salt. It teaches about the chemical properties of salt, the history of salt, and uses for this important chemical.

Experiments

Chemistry Experiments You Can Do at Home!

http://chemistry.about.com/od/homeexperiments/

This site has many experiments you can do at home. Although it is directed at high school chemistry students, many of the activities use common materials and would not be difficult to do in your kitchen or garage. Experiments include making smoke machines and growing salt crystals.

Molecules and Atoms

Library of 3-D Molecular Structures
http://honiglab.cpmc.columbia.edu/grasp/pictures.html

Molecular Art Gallery
http://www.wag.caltech.edu/gallery/art_gallery.html
These sites have beautiful color images of molecules. Although they are advanced, you may find the explanations and pictures useful if you are studying molecules.

Life, the Universe, and the Electron
http://www.sciencemuseum.org.uk/on-line/electron/index.asp
This Web site celebrates the one-hundredth anniversary of the discovery of the electron. It tells what electrons are, how we know about them, and what they mean to modern scientists.

MicroWorlds: Exploring the Structure of Materials
http://www.lbl.gov/MicroWorlds/
Scientists use a machine called the advanced light source (ALS) to learn about atoms and molecules. In MicroWorlds you can learn how the ALS works and what it tells us about matter.

Periodic Tables

ChemicalElements.com
http://www.chemicalelements.com/

Chemicool Periodic Table
http://www.chemicool.com/

Los Alamos Periodic Table
http://periodic.lanl.gov/

Periodic Table of Comic Books
http://www.uky.edu/Projects/Chemcomics/

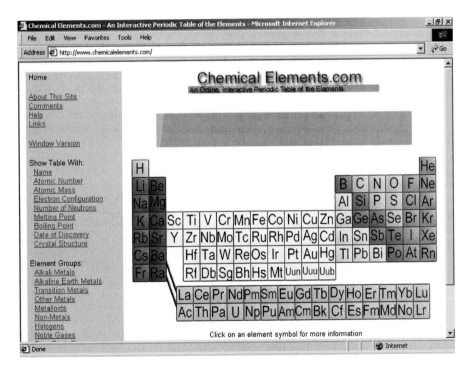

A periodic table of the elements, many of which can be found on the Internet, is helpful for many chemistry projects.

Chapter 8

Physics Projects Using the Internet

Christopher had a pendulum cuckoo clock in his room. He could adjust the speed of the clock by moving the weight on the pendulum. This made him curious. He wondered about the relationship between length and time for the pendulum. And what about other variables? How would changing the mass of the pendulum affect the speed of the clock? Since he had to complete a science fair project, he decided to construct an experiment to answer these questions.

To prepare for his research, Christopher searched the Internet for information that would relate to the pendulum. He visited the

How Things Work Search Page
http://howthingswork.virginia.edu/
to see whether anyone had asked about the pendulum before him.

He then did a search for "pendulum," and several questions and answers came up. Some were quite useful to him. One question and answer defined some important terms for him, such as *period, amplitude,* and *frequency.*

Christopher also found this pendulum-related site:

Virtual Labs & Simulations: Simple Harmonic Motion

http://www.hazelwood.k12.mo.us/~grichert/sciweb/shm.htm

What he then saw inspired him. This site included a variety of simulations of springs and pendulums. Christopher could change such variables as the stiffness and the mass of the

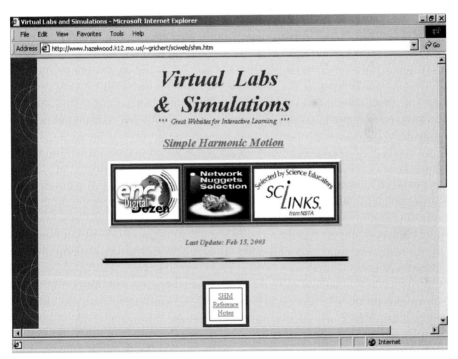

Christopher looked at the Virtual Labs & Simulations site, which included many simulations of pendulums and springs.

spring. After playing with the controls for a while, he started to realize that certain patterns existed. For instance, long pendulums move slower than short ones, but changing the mass of the pendulum does not affect its period (the time to swing back and forth once).

Christopher built an actual pendulum to explore the relationship between the length and period of the pendulum. He set the length of the pendulum to 0.2 meters. He timed how long it took for the pendulum to swing back and forth ten times, to the nearest tenth of a second. He set up a table for his data.

LENGTH (m)	10 SWINGS (s)	1 SWING (s)
0.20	17.5	1.75
0.40		
0.60		

DO NOT WRITE IN THIS BOOK.

The first column gives the length of the pendulum in meters. Christopher hung the pendulum from a pipe near the ceiling for the longer lengths. The second column is the time required for ten swings, which he recorded with a stopwatch to the nearest tenth of a second. The third column is simply the number in the second column divided by ten. Christopher's purpose of timing ten swings and then dividing by ten was to reduce the human error in timing. He took all his measurements, from 0.2 m to 2.0 m, and completed the table. Then he graphed time as a function of length. His graph showed that as the pendulum got longer, the time it took to swing back and forth was also longer. When he made this type of adjustment on his cuckoo clock, it ran slower. This made sense after his experiment.

Christopher changed his experiment design. This time, instead of changing the length of the pendulum, he changed the mass and kept the length constant. His table headings looked like this:

MASS (g)	10 SWINGS (s)	1 SWING (s)

What he found was a little surprising, but it agreed with the simple harmonic motion simulation: The period of the pendulum did *not* change with mass. The resulting graph of time as a function of mass was merely a horizontal line.

Christopher tried changing the amplitude of the swing—how far he pulled the pendulum to the side—to see how that affected the period. Amplitude, too, had no effect on the period.

Using his experimental data, combined with theories and historical information he found on the Web, Christopher determined that the only factors that affected the period of the pendulum are length and the gravitational pull of the earth. (Air resistance was a minor force and barely had any effect on the pendulum.) He also found that the pendulum and the spring move according to simple harmonic motion, which is common in nature and technology and important to scientists and engineers.

Other Sites to Help You in Your Physics Research

Density, Buoyancy, Fluids, and Air Forces

Air Travelers

http://www.omsi.edu/visit/physics/air/

Air Travelers is a site dedicated to the science of hot-air balloons. You can learn about gas properties and buoyancy from the information and activities provided there. The site is designed for teachers, but the Balloon Activities section may give you some project ideas.

Dragonfly Flight Activities

http://www.units.muohio.edu/dragonfly/flight/flight_contents.htmlx

You can build paper airplanes and design a human-powered plane at this site.

NASA's Aerodynamics in Car Racing

http://www.nas.nasa.gov/About/Education/Racecar/aerodynamics.html

This site discusses the aerodynamics that engineers must understand when they design race cars. The Bernoulli effect results when air rushes over a surface. This important effect helps race car drivers control their vehicles. It also provides lift to airplane wings.

The Science of Ballooning

http://www.pbs.org/wgbh/nova/balloon/science/

This is another site dedicated to ballooning. It gives the history of ballooning and discusses atmospheric science. An excellent section describes the jet stream.

Water Works

http://www.omsi.edu/visit/physics/ww/

WaterWorks is devoted to the science of fountains. Fountains are an artistic and practical part of our environment. This site gives instructions on investigating fountains and creating your own designs.

General Physics Sites

Energy Quest

http://www.EnergyQuest.ca.gov

Energy Quest is an award-winning site from the California Energy Commission. You can learn all about energy: the different forms of energy, uses of energy, and conservation of energy. It also covers topics such as alternative-fuel vehicles and geothermal energy.

Flash Animations for Physics

http://www.upscale.utoronto.ca/

Using physics animations, this site covers a wide range of topics such as waves, optics, and electricity.

Glenbrook South Physics Home Page

http://www.glenbrook.k12.il.us/gbssci/phys/phys.html

This site contains lessons, theories, and simulations. Explore the pages at this site to see if you can find a project that suits your interests. You can visit their multimedia physics studios to see animations of trains, falling objects, rockets, and satellites. There is a special physics projects area that includes studies of roller coasters, egg drops, traffic, potential energy, heat, acoustics, astronomy, sports, sailing, relativity, and flight.

MyPhysicsLab Physics Simulations with Java

http://www.myphysicslab.com/

If you have a Java-enabled browser, this is a fascinating site. There are simulations of springs, blocks, and molecules. If you try a general Web search for physics simulations, many Java- and Shockwave-using sites will come up. You can conduct virtual "thought" experiments, much in the way Einstein developed his laws of relativity.

Nano World: Scale and Magnification

http://www.uq.edu.au/nanoworld/scalemag.html

This site is all about scale and magnification. You will see the relative sizes of some familiar objects. Measurement is very important in physics, and length is one of the fundamental quantities.

U.S. Navy Time Service Department

http://tycho.usno.navy.mil/frontpage.html

Time is another fundamental quantity in physics. At this site you can get the exact time from the U.S. Naval Observatory Master Clock. Find out how the clock works and what other functions are served by the Time Service Department.

Mechanics and Engineering

The Exploratorium's Sport Science Exhibit

http://www.exploratorium.edu/sports/index.html

This site deals with all aspects of the physics of sports. You can learn about cycling, including the importance of frame materials, friction, gears, aerodynamics, and design and racing strategies. The San Jose Sharks helped the Exploratorium create the hockey exhibit. It deals with friction, reaction time, and collisions. Other sports profiled include baseball, skateboarding, and surfing.

Java Projectile Motion

http://www.upscale.utoronto.ca/GeneralInterest/Harrison/
Flash/ClassMechanics/Projectile/Projectile.html

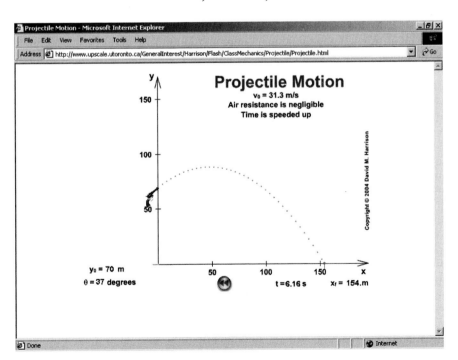

This graph was generated on the Java Projectile Motion site.

This site requires a browser feature called Java. If you have Java installed on your computer, you can do simulations of projectile motion. You can vary the position and angle to see where the projectiles land. You can print images of the different paths of projectiles and their graphs.

Amusement Park Physics: Design a Roller Coaster

http://www.learner.org/exhibits/parkphysics/coaster.html

This fun site contains information about the history and physics of roller coasters. It teaches how roller coasters actually work, and includes a glossary of important physics terms. You can design a roller coaster and find out how the laws of physics influence ride design.

Design your own roller coaster using the principles of physics.

Waves, Light, and Electromagnetism

About Rainbows

http://eo.ucar.edu/rainbows/

What is a rainbow? How are rainbows formed? What are the parts of a rainbow? When can you see them? The answers can be found at this award-winning site.

The Atoms Family

http://www.miamisci.org/af/sln/

The Atoms Family is a clever site about energy, particle physics, waves, electricity, and other topics in theoretical physics. Visit Dracula's Library, Frankenstein's Lightning Laboratory, and other scary rooms.

Bob Miller's Light Walk

http://www.exploratorium.edu/light_walk/index.html

Bob Miller is an artist, and the San Francisco Exploratorium hosts an online exhibit for him. Activities are also provided. You can do your own "light walk," make a pinhole camera, and try slide projector activities.

The Frank DeFreitas Holography Studio

http://www.enter.net/~holostudio/

Enter the studio for educational resources on holograms. HoloKids is for elementary-level students. You will find out what holograms are and how to make your own hologram portraits; hear a hologram radio show; and find links to other hologram sites.

Making Waves: An Online Guide to Sound and Electromagnetic Radiation

http://www.smgaels.org/physics/home.htm

This is an online science project completed by St. Mary's School in Manhasset, New York. You can explore all the different wavelengths of radiation and sound. Learn about light, microwaves, X-rays, and other forms of radiation and wave energy.

NASA ScIenceFiles: Electricity Activities

http://scifiles.larc.nasa.gov/text/kids/D_Lab/acts_electric.html

Age-appropriate activities you can try in electricity.

The Particle Adventure

http://particleadventure.org/particleadventure/

This site leads you through a tour of subatomic particles and explains the historical development of theoretical physics. Use the resources here to do a project that teaches how scientists discovered what they know about the organization of matter.

Science Made Simple: What Is Static Electricity?

http://www.sciencemadesimple.com/static.html

This is a tutorial on static electricity. A shocking site!

Further Reading

Bombaugh, Ruth. *Science Fair Success, Revised and Expanded.* Springfield, N.J.: Enslow Publishers, Inc., 1999.

Gardner, Robert. *Science Fair Projects—Planning, Presenting, Succeeding.* Berkeley Heights, N.J.: Enslow Publishers, Inc., 1999.

———. *Science Fair Success Revised and Expanded.* Berkeley Heights, N.J.: Enslow Publishers, Inc., 1999.

Parks, Peggy J. *The Internet.* San Diego, Calif.: Kidhaven Press, 2004.

Rosner, Marc. *The Scientific American Book of Great Science Fair Projects.* Hoboken, N.J.: Wiley, 2000.

Staff of DK Publishing and Staff of Google. *e.encyclopedia Science.* New York: DK Publishing, Inc., 2004.

Index